EMOTIONAL MAN

Mandalas have been used for centuries across various cultures, symbolizing wholeness, balance, and harmony. From intricate designs in sacred rituals to modern interpretations in art and therapy, mandalas hold a special significance. They serve as visual representations of the universe, offering a path toward inner peace and mindfulness. In recent years, the act of coloring mandalas has been recognized for its therapeutic benefits, helping people relieve stress, foster creativity, and process emotions.

This book, "Emotional Mandalas," goes beyond simple coloring. It connects the act of art-making with emotional awareness, allowing you to choose a mandala that resonates with how you're feeling in the moment. Through coloring, you'll not only express yourself but also gain a deeper understanding of your emotions. Each mandala in this book is paired with a particular emotion, offering guidance on how to navigate your emotional landscape.

Whether you're feeling joyful, anxious, peaceful, or anything in between, this book invites you to use art as a way to process, reflect, and transform. Let's embark on this colorful journey of emotional exploration and healing together.

Tips for Your Emotional Mandalas

1. **Embrace Your Style:** There's no right or wrong way to complete a mandala. Feel free to express yourself, whether it's with meticulous detail or broad, sweeping strokes.
2. **Find Your Flow:** Let the process of drawing and coloring be meditative. Focus on the movements of your hand and the texture of the paper to find a rhythm that's soothing and personal to you.
3. **Experiment with Colors:** Colors can influence mood and emotion. Experiment with different color schemes to see how they reflect your feelings and thoughts during the coloring process.
4. **Use the Right Tools:** While you can start with any pencil or pen, experimenting with different thicknesses and types (like fine liners or gel pens) can add a new dimension to your artwork.
5. **Take Breaks:** If you find yourself getting lost in the details or feeling overwhelmed, it's okay to take a break. Your mandala will be there when you're ready to return.
6. **There are No Mistakes:** If you go outside the lines or a pattern doesn't turn out as you planned, embrace it. Every unique touch adds character and personal meaning to your mandala.
7. **Layer Your Work:** Feel free to add layers to your drawing. Starting with lighter colors and adding darker shades can create depth and richness in your design.
8. **Set the Mood:** Create a relaxing environment while you color. Maybe light a candle, play some soft music, or enjoy a cup of tea as you work.
9. **Reflect on Your Journey:** After completing a mandala, take a moment to reflect on the experience. What did you feel while coloring? What does the finished piece say to you?
10. **Share Your Art:** If you feel comfortable, share your completed mandalas with friends or family, or on social media. Every piece is a reflection of your journey and can be a source of inspiration to others.

Color this mandala if you're feeling

Joyful

Embrace the sunshine within. Let your joy light up the world.

Color this mandala if you're feeling

Sad

*It's okay to feel sad.
Every tear is a step toward healing.*

Color this mandala if you're feeling

Excited

Let your excitement be the spark that ignites your passion.

Color this mandala if you're feeling

Anxious

Breathe in peace, exhale worry.
You are stronger than your fears.

Color this mandala if you're feeling

Peaceful

May tranquility fill your heart and calm your soul.

Color this mandala if you're feeling

Angry

Channel your anger into strength. Let it fuel positive change.

Color this mandala if you're feeling

Hopeful

Hold onto hope. It's the beacon guiding you forward.

Color this mandala if you're feeling

Lonely

You are not alone. Reach out and connection will find you.

Color this mandala if you're feeling

Grateful

Let gratitude fill your heart, illuminating life's blessings.

Color this mandala if you're feeling

Frustrated

This too shall pass. Clarity follows confusion.

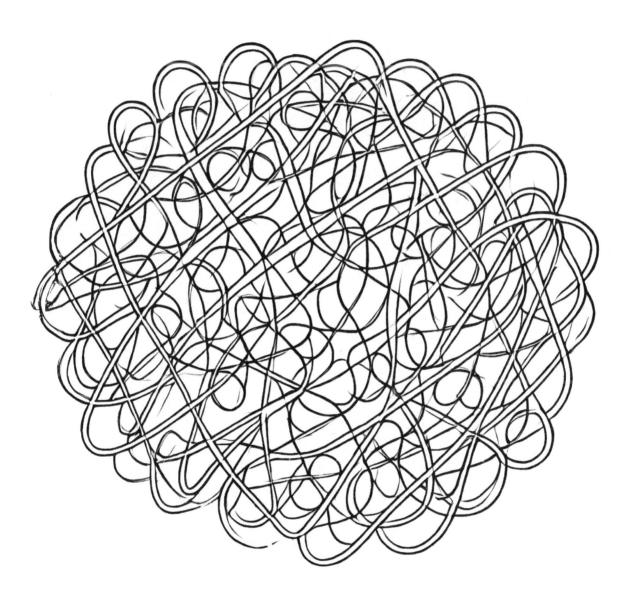

Color this mandala if you're feeling

Inspired

Let inspiration lift you. Your ideas have the power to soar.

Color this mandala if you're feeling

Bored

In stillness, creativity awaits to be awakened.

Color this mandala if you're feeling

Confident

Believe in yourself. You are capable and strong.

Color this mandala if you're feeling

Scared

Courage doesn't mean you don't get afraid. It means you don't let fear stop you.

Color this mandala if you're feeling

Content

Savor the peace of this moment.
All is well.

Color this mandala if you're feeling

Disappointed

Every ending is a new beginning in disguise.

Color this mandala if you're feeling

Curious

Let your curiosity lead you to new horizons.

Color this mandala if you're feeling

Guilty

Forgive yourself. Growth begins with acceptance.

Color this mandala if you're feeling

Relaxed

Let go and unwind. Serenity is within reach.

Color this mandala if you're feeling

Overwhelmed

Take it one step at a time. You've got this.

Color this mandala if you're feeling

Proud

Be proud of how far you've come and all you've accomplished.

Color this mandala if you're feeling

Jealous

Transform envy into motivation for your own journey.

Color this mandala if you're feeling

Energetic

Embrace your vitality. Let it move you forward.

Color this mandala if you're feeling

Exhausted

Rest is not a luxury. It's essential for renewal.

Color this mandala if you're feeling

Loving

Love freely and fully. It is the greatest gift of all.

Color this mandala if you're feeling

Hurt

Healing takes time. Be gentle with yourself.

Color this mandala if you're feeling

Hurt

Healing takes time. Be gentle with yourself.

Color this mandala if you're feeling

Optimistic

Look ahead with hope. Wonderful things are coming.

Color this mandala if you're feeling

Ashamed

Release the weight of shame. You are deserving of compassion.

Color this mandala if you're feeling

Playful

Let your inner child run free and enjoy the moment.

Color this mandala if you're feeling

Stressed

Pause and breathe. Ttranquility is just a moment away.

Color this mandala if you're feeling

Forgiving

Forgiveness liberates the soul. Let go and find peace.

Color this mandala if you're feeling

Cheerful

Share your smile. It's contagious and brightens the day.

Color this mandala if you're feeling

Empathetic

Your understanding brings comfort to those around you.

Color this mandala if you're feeling

Indifferent

It's okay to take a step back. Give yourself space.

Color this mandala if you're feeling

Amused

Find joy in the little things that make you smile.

Color this mandala if you're feeling

Nervous

Embrace the butterflies. They mean you're alive.

Color this mandala if you're feeling

Secure

You are safe and protected. Trust in your foundation.

Color this mandala if you're feeling

Vulnerable

There is strength in openness. It's the gateway to connection.

We would love to hear about your experience with this coloring book, and we would greatly appreciate it if you could leave a review to help spread the word to other potential people who need this.

Thank you so much!

Any questions, feel free to write to
ericabillstorm@gmail.com

Printed in Great Britain
by Amazon